I Can Read Music

a note reading book for VIOLIN students

by Joanne Martin

Volume 2

Copyright © 1997 Summy-Birchard Music
Division of Summy-Birchard Inc.
All rights reserved. Printed in U.S.A.

ISBN 0-87487-427-0

Summy-Birchard Inc.
exclusively distributed by
Warner Bros. Publications
15800 N.W. 48th Avenue, Miami, FL 33014
All rights reserved   Printed in U.S.A.

The Suzuki name, logo and wheel device
are trademarks of Dr. Shinichi Suzuki used
under exclusive license by Summy-Birchard, Inc.

I CAN READ MUSIC VOLUME II

I Can Read Music Volume II is the second in a series of music reading books designed for Suzuki-trained students, but which are useful also in other string teaching contexts.

A student who has completed the first book in this series, or who has previous music reading experience, is ready for this second book. I recommend a minimum playing level equivalent to the end of *Suzuki Violin School Volume II*.

Rhythm and pitch were taught separately in *I Can Read Music Volume I*, and are reviewed and combined in *Volume II*. Other time signatures and keys are introduced, using additional finger patterns in first position. Since most exercises build on previously introduced material, I recommend moving through the book in sequence. Most pages are set up as duets, with the parts of equal difficulty. Playing the duets with a teacher, parent, or another student will prepare the student for chamber music.

My goal in teaching note reading is to enable students to hear music in their heads when they see the printed page. When we read a story out loud, we glance ahead and grasp the sense of upcoming words, then we can read expressively. The same idea is true in music reading. I believe that we can teach students to recognize musical symbols as representing sounds. Fragments of familiar melodies appear throughout this book. Once the student recognizes the melody, the tune and/or rhythm should be obvious. However, many melodies contain a surprise, to ensure that the eye and the ear work together.

Rhythmic reading is essential to strong sight reading. Most students concentrate on which pitch to play, and need help to develop their ability to play rhythmically. In this book I have presented rhythmic patterns using the Twinkle Variations from the *Suzuki Violin School Volume I*. These variations prepare the student to read off-beats, syncopations and dotted rhythms.

I believe that musicians ought to be able to count out loud while sight reading. It is worth taking the time to develop this ability. If students can walk the pulse while playing and can count out loud while playing a simple review piece, they easily learn to count out loud while reading.

Visual grouping of beats is important to strong reading. Pointing to the beginning of each beat while singing (using note names or a syllable such as "la") trains the eye to see beat units. Throughout *I Can Read Music Volume II* rhythmic patterns are drawn in boxes. A half note box is twice as wide as a quarter, etc. This system corresponds to the flash cards which many teachers use for rhythmic reading. Seeing beats and beat groups on these cards helps develop rhythmic reading much faster than talking about fractions. Students may not understand mathematically why four sixteenth notes equal one quarter note, but they quickly learn to feel the grouping when those four sixteenths take up the same size card as one quarter note.

Learning to read music is a natural and essential stage in a musician's training. By connecting the printed page with sounds they can already play, students can take advantage of their ear for music and become strong and confident readers.

ACKNOWLEDGMENTS

I Can Read Music Volume II has evolved with the guidance of many colleagues and students, who generously gave their time to help me simplify and clarify what I have written. I owe special thanks to my daughter Shauna, who started me on writing note reading books, and who has helped me to understand the unique musical thought processes of a Suzuki-trained student. Thanks also to my sister Patricia Martin Shand for her invaluable advice and wisdom. This book is dedicated to my husband Peter for his ongoing patience and support. He played through all the materials, in several draft versions, on violin, viola and cello, constantly encouraging me with his sense of humour and love of music.

Joanne Martin

REFERENCE GUIDE

SEQUENCE IN WHICH NEW MATERIAL IS PRESENTED

TIME SIGNATURES

QUARTER NOTE BEATS

4/4	Lesson 1
3/4	Lesson 2
5/4	Lesson 4
2/4	Lesson 6
C	Lesson 10

HALF NOTE BEATS

2/2	Lesson 55
¢	Lesson 58
3/2	Lesson 59
4/2	Lesson 62

EIGHTH NOTE BEATS

3/8	Lesson 72
4/8	Lesson 75
5/8	Lesson 78

COMPOUND TIME

6/8	Lesson 88
9/8	Lesson 94
12/8	Lesson 97

RHYTHMS

SIMPLE TIME

♩	Lesson 1
♪	Lesson 1
♩.	Lesson 2
o	Lesson 3
♩	Lesson 4
♫	Lesson 6
—	Lesson 7
	Lesson 16
	Lesson 20
	Lesson 20
	Lesson 29
	Lesson 32
	Lesson 35
	Lesson 37
	Lesson 41
	Lesson 43
	Lesson 49
o·	Lesson 60
	Lesson 62
	Lesson 87

RHYTHMS

COMPOUND TIME

♩.	Lesson 88
♩.	Lesson 88
	Lesson 88
	Lesson 88
	Lesson 90
	Lesson 92

BOWING MARKINGS

⊓	Downbow	Lesson 11
V	Upbow	Lesson 12
	Tie	Lesson 43
	Slur	Lesson 53
	Linked bow	Lesson 61
,	Lift and reset	Lesson 63

KEYS and FINGER PATTERNS (in first position)

A MAJOR	Key signature		Lesson 3
	1 octave scale (starting open A)	2-3 close	Lesson 8
	1 octave scale (starting 1 on G)	high 3	Lesson 65
	2 octave scale	high 3/regular 3	Lesson 67
D MAJOR	Key signature		Lesson 13
	1 octave scale (starting open D)	2-3 close	Lesson 15
	Scale passage (open D to 3 on E)	low 2/high 2	Lesson 39
	Scale passage (1 on G to 3 on A)	high 3/regular 3	Lesson 70
G MAJOR	Key signature		Lesson 22
	1 octave scale (starting open G)	2-3 close	Lesson 23
	1 octave scale (starting 3 on D)	low 2	Lesson 25
	2 octave scale	low 2/high 2	Lesson 27
C MAJOR	Key signature		Lesson 46
	1 octave scale (starting 3 on G)	low 2	Lesson 46
	Scale passage (open G to 2 on A)	low 2/high 2	Lesson 48
	Scale passage (2 on A to 3 on E)	low 1	Lesson 81
	Scale passage (3 on G to 2 on E)	low 1/regular 1	Lesson 95
F MAJOR	Key signature		Lesson 83
	1 octave scale (starting 2 on D)	low 1	Lesson 83

I CAN READ MUSIC VOLUME II   TEACHERS' NOTES

New material is introduced in the order listed below. Lessons not mentioned here review previously presented material.

New pitches or finger patterns are introduced in scale passages, using accidentals rather than key signatures. I suggest that the student sing each line of music before playing it, using a reference pitch so that the sung pitch corresponds with the pitch which will be played on the violin. In this book finger numbers only appear when pitches are first introduced. I recommend that pitches be identified by letter names rather than by finger numbers.

New rhythms are first introduced on open strings. I suggest that before playing an exercise, the student point to each beat (not the subdivision of the beat) and count out loud or sing. Pointing helps keep the pulse steady, develops recognition of patterns such as groups of eighth or sixteenth notes, and emphasizes the rhythmic values of rests.

1. E string notes (E F# G# A)

    ♩ ♩

    4/4 time signature

2. Duets

    ♩.

    3/4 time signature

3. A major key signature

    o

4. Key signatures are used from here on, except when new pitches or finger patterns are presented.

    𝄽

    5/4 time signature

5. A string notes (A B C# D)

6.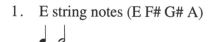

    2/4 time signature

7. ▬

8. A major scale (1 octave starting on open A)

10. c = **4/4**

11. Downbow ⊓

12. Upbow V

13. Notes on the D string (D E F# G)
     D major key signature

15. D major scale (1 octave starting on open D)

16. ♫♫♩♩ "Twinkle" Variation A

18. Duet parts have different rhythms

20. ♫ ♩ ⁊ ♪ "Twinkle" Variation B

     ⁊

22. Notes on the G string (G A B C)
     G major key signature

23. G major scale (1 octave starting on open G)

25. G major scale (1 octave starting on 3rd finger on D string)
     - low 2nd finger

27. G major scale (2 octaves starting on open G)
     - high 2nd and low 2nd fingers

29. ♩ ♫ ♩ ♫ "Twinkle" Variation C

32. ♫♩

35. ♪♫ "Twinkle" B reversed

37. Offbeats ♪♪

39. D major scale (starting on open D, extended to E string)
    - high 2nd and low 2nd finger

41. ♩ ♪

43. Dotted notes ♩. = ♩♪

46. C major scale (1 octave starting on 3rd finger on G string)
    C major key signature

48. C major scale (extended down to G string)
    - high 2nd and low 2nd finger

49. Syncopation ♪♩♪

53. Slurs

55. $\frac{2}{2}$ time signature

    The same melodies are notated in $\frac{2}{4}$ and $\frac{2}{2}$

    to help the student hear half note beats.

58. ¢ = $\frac{2}{2}$

59. $\frac{3}{2}$ time signature

    The same melodies are notated in $\frac{3}{4}$ and $\frac{3}{2}$

60. 𝅝·

61. Linked bowing

62. ⫶

    $\frac{4}{2}$ time signature

63. Lift and reset the bow ,

65. A major scale (1 octave starting on 1st finger on G string)
    - high 3rd finger

67. A major scale (2 octaves starting on 1st finger on G string)
    - high 3rd and regular 3rd finger

69. Duet taking two lines. The student will need to learn to read
    ahead to be ready for the second line.

70. D major scale (extended down to G string)
    - high 3rd and regular 3rd finger

72. $\frac{3}{8}$ time signature

    The same melodies are notated in $\frac{3}{4}$ and $\frac{3}{8}$

75. $\frac{4}{8}$ time signature

    The same melodies are notated in $\frac{4}{4}$ and $\frac{4}{8}$

78. $\frac{5}{8}$ time signature

    The same melodies are notated in $\frac{5}{4}$ and $\frac{5}{8}$

81. F ♮ (low 1st finger on the E string)

83. F major scale (starting on 2nd finger on D string)
    F major key signature

87. ♫♩

88. $\frac{6}{8}$ time signature

    The same melodies are notated in $\frac{2}{4}$ with triplets and in $\frac{6}{8}$

94. $\frac{9}{8}$ time signature

95. C major scale (starting on 3rd on G, extended to E string)
    - low 1st and regular 1st finger

97. $\frac{12}{8}$ time signature

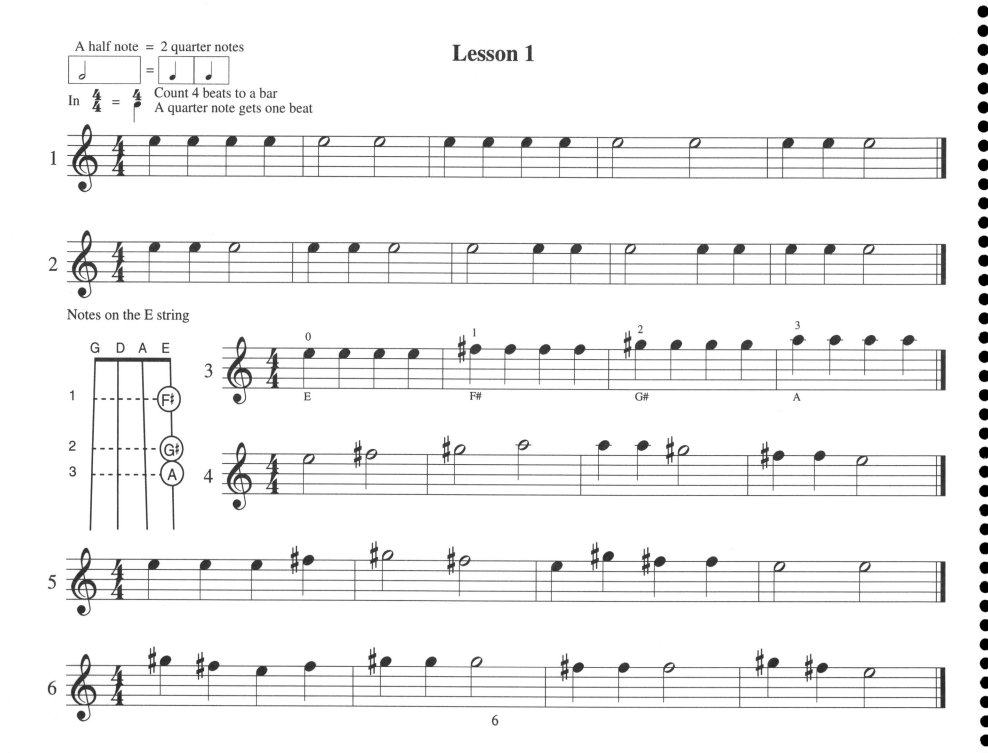

A dotted half note = 3 quarter notes

Lesson 2

In $\frac{3}{4}$ = Count 3 beats to a bar. A quarter note gets one beat

Play these lines as duets

7

Lesson 3

A whole note = 4 quarter notes

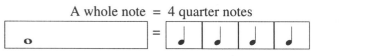

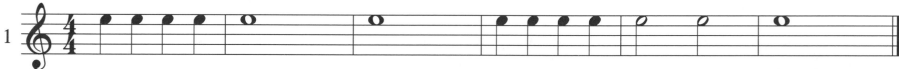

These pairs of lines sound the same
Lines 4 and 6 use a key signature instead of accidentals
The key signature of A major has three sharps (F# C# and G#)

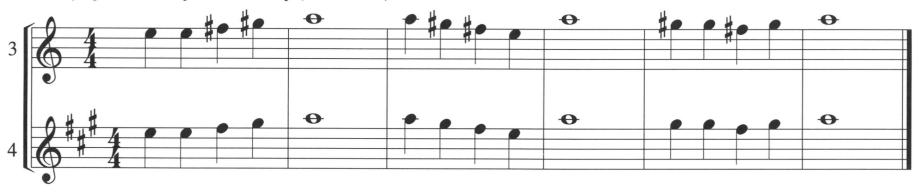

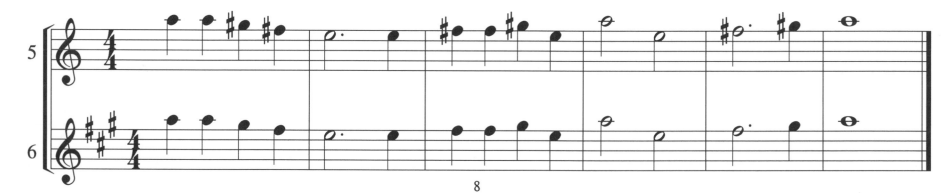

A quarter rest = a silent quarter note

Lesson 4

In $\frac{5}{4}$ = $\frac{5}{4}$ Count 5 beats to a bar
A quarter note gets one beat

Each pair of lines sounds the same

9

Lesson 5

Notes on the A string

Play these lines as duets

10

Lesson 6

2 eighth notes = 1 quarter note

Count 2 beats to a bar
A quarter note gets one beat

Play these lines as duets

Lesson 7

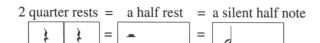

2 quarter rests = a half rest = a silent half note

12

Lesson 8

Lesson 9

14

Lesson 10

$\frac{4}{4}$ is sometimes written as **C**

C is called "common time"

Lesson 11

means play downbow

16

Lesson 12

17

Lesson 13

Notes on the D string

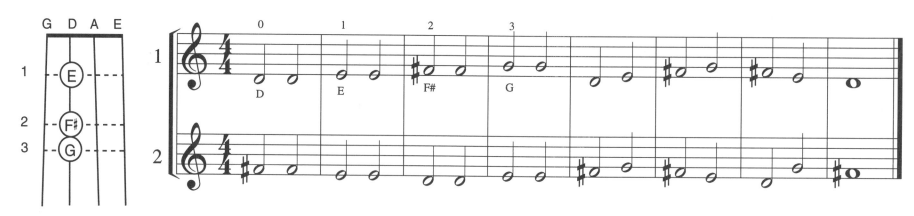

The key signature of D major has 2 sharps (F# and C#)

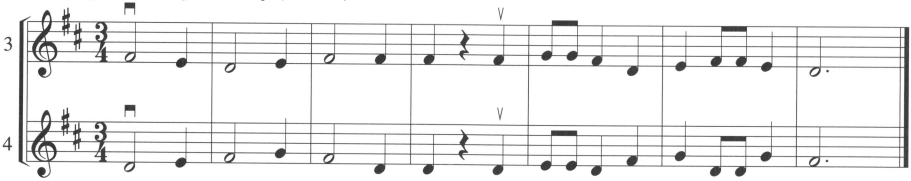

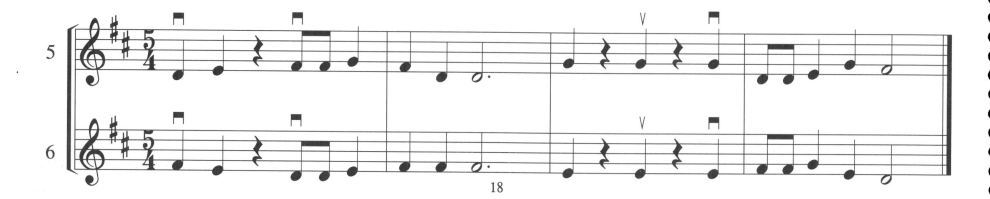

18

Lesson 14

19

Lesson 15

20

Lesson 17

22

Lesson 18

Each duet part has a different rhythm

23

Lesson 19

24

An eighth rest = a silent eighth note

Lesson 20

is like "Twinkle" Variation B

25

Lesson 21

26

Lesson 22

Notes on the G string

The key signature G major has 1 sharp (F#)

27

Lesson 23

Lesson 24

29

Lesson 25

In G major scale
Low 2 on A and E strings (for C and G)

30

Lesson 26

31

Lesson 27

In G major scale two octaves
   High 2 on G and D strings (for B and F#)
   Low 2 on A and E strings (for C and G)

32

Lesson 28

Remember - in G major
High 2 on G and D strings (for B and F#)
Low 2 on A and E strings (for C and G)

33

An eighth and 2 sixteenth notes = 1 quarter note

Lesson 29

34

Lesson 30

35

Lesson 31

36

Lesson 33

38

Lesson 34

Remember the rhythms ♫ and ♫

Remember A major (see Lesson 8)

39

Lesson 35

Lesson 36

Remember - an eighth rest is a silent eighth note

41

Lesson 37

Remember D major (see Lesson 15)

42

Lesson 38

43

Lesson 39

In D major
High 2 on D and A strings (for F# and C#)
Low 2 on E string (for G)

44

Lesson 40

Remember - in D major
   High 2 on D and A strings (for F# and C#)
   Low 2 on E string (for G)

45

Lesson 41

Remember - an eighth rest is a silent eighth note

Lesson 42

Remember G major (see Lesson 27)

47

Lesson 43

A dotted quarter note = a quarter note tied to an eighth note

A tie joins two notes of the same pitch

The tied notes become one single note, held as long as the two notes added together

Each pair of lines sounds the same

48

Lesson 44

49

Lesson 45

50

Lesson 46

In C major scale
Low 2 on D and A strings (for F and C)

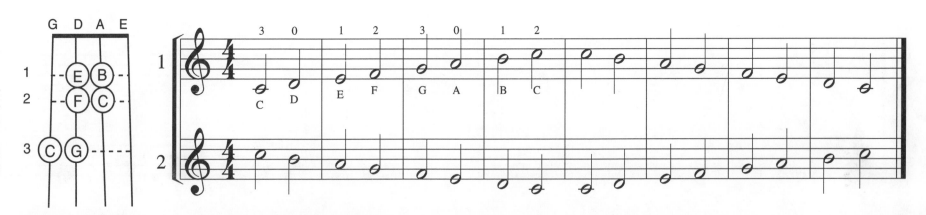

The key signature of C major has no sharps or flats

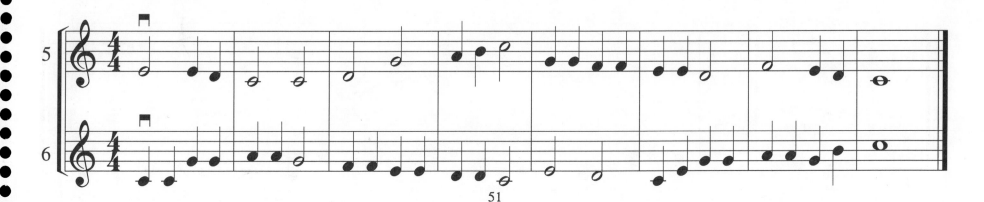

51

Lesson 47

52

Lesson 48

In C major
Low 2 on A and D strings (for C and F)
High 2 on G string (for B)

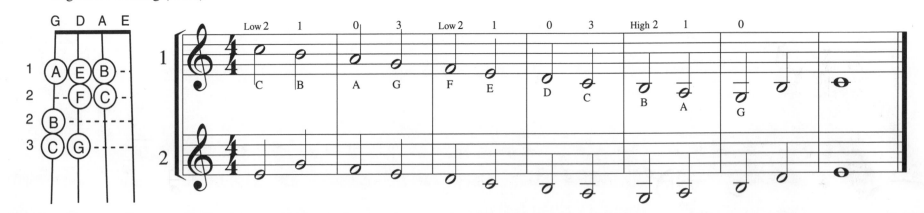

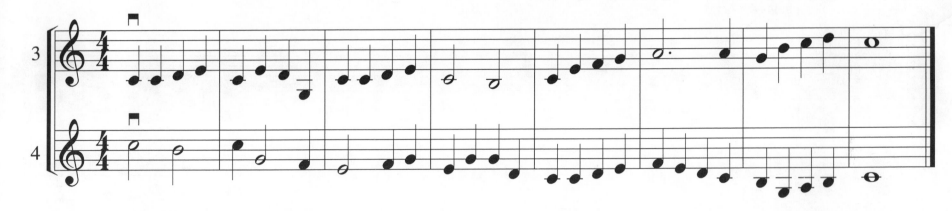

Lesson 49

Remember - a tie joins notes together
so they sound like one note

Clap rhythm- Count out loud & clap.

Each pair of lines sounds the same

54

Lesson 50

55

Lesson 51

Remember G major (see Lesson 27)

56

Lesson 52

Remember - in G major
High 2 on G and D strings (for B and F#)
Low 2 on A and E strings (for C and G)

A slur tells you to play 2 or more notes in the same bow

A slur affects the direction of the bow
not the length of the notes

Lesson 53

Lesson 54

59

In $\frac{2}{2}$ = $\frac{2}{\text{♩}}$ Count 2 beats to a bar
A half note gets one beat

Lesson 55

Count 2 beats to a bar in $\frac{2}{4}$ and $\frac{2}{2}$
Each pair of lines sounds the same

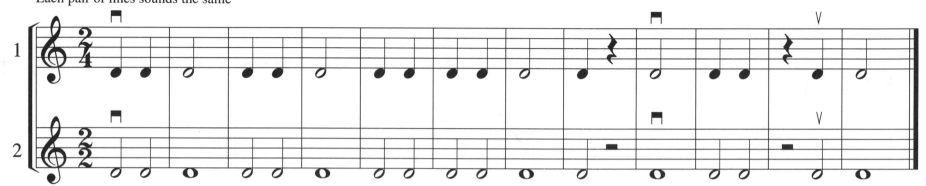

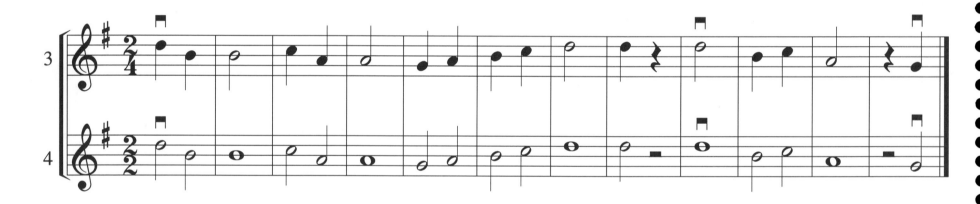

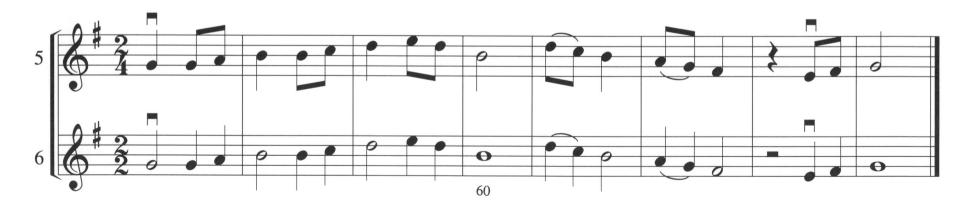

Rhythm
Pitch.
Bowing

Lesson 56

Remember - count 2 beats to a bar in $\frac{2}{4}$ and $\frac{2}{2}$

Lesson 57

Remember

In **2/2** = **2/2** (half note)   Count two beats to a bar
                            A half note gets one beat

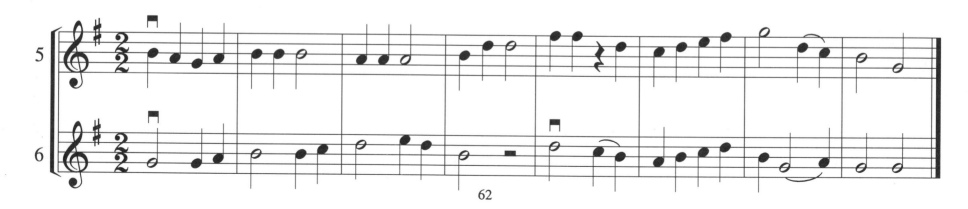

Lesson 58

2/2 is sometimes written as

¢ is called "alla breve" or "cut time"

63

In $\frac{3}{2}$ = $\frac{3}{\text{\textohalf}}$ Count 3 beats to a bar
                                                A half note gets one beat

Count 3 beats to a bar in $\frac{3}{4}$ and $\frac{3}{2}$
Each pair of lines sounds the same

Lesson 59

Lesson 60

A dotted whole note = 3 half notes

Remember C major (see Lesson 48)

65

Rhythm Letters

♩ ♩ means play a slur, stopping between the notes

Lesson 61

This is called linked bowing

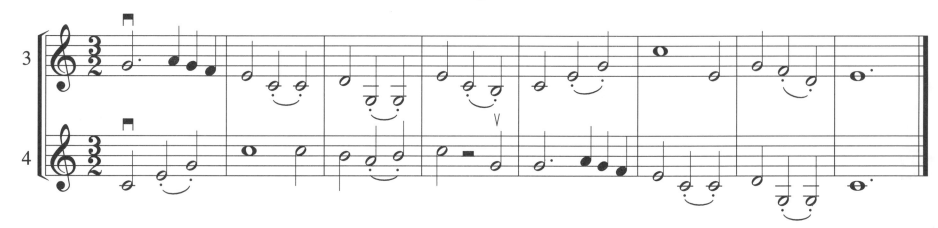

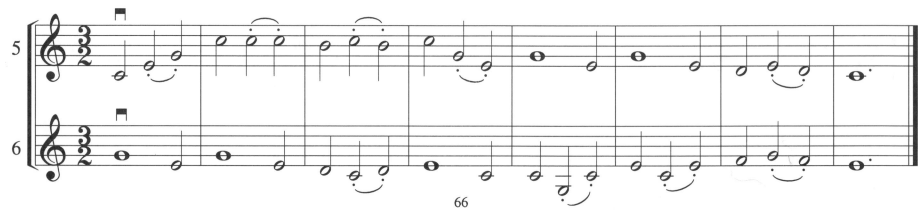

A breve (double whole note) = 4 half notes

In 4/2 = Count 4 beats to a bar
A half note gets one beat

Lesson 62

67

Lesson 63

, means lift and reset the bow
Remember G major (see Lesson 27)

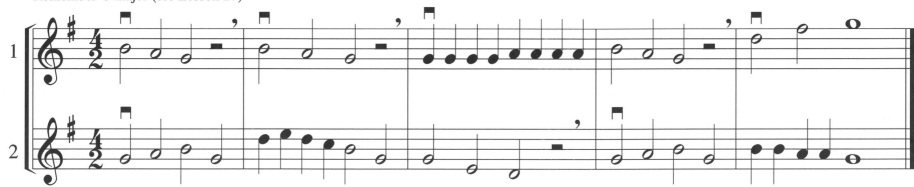

The rest of this page is one duet
Read ahead when you reach the end of the line

68

Lesson 64

Remember D major (see Lesson 39)

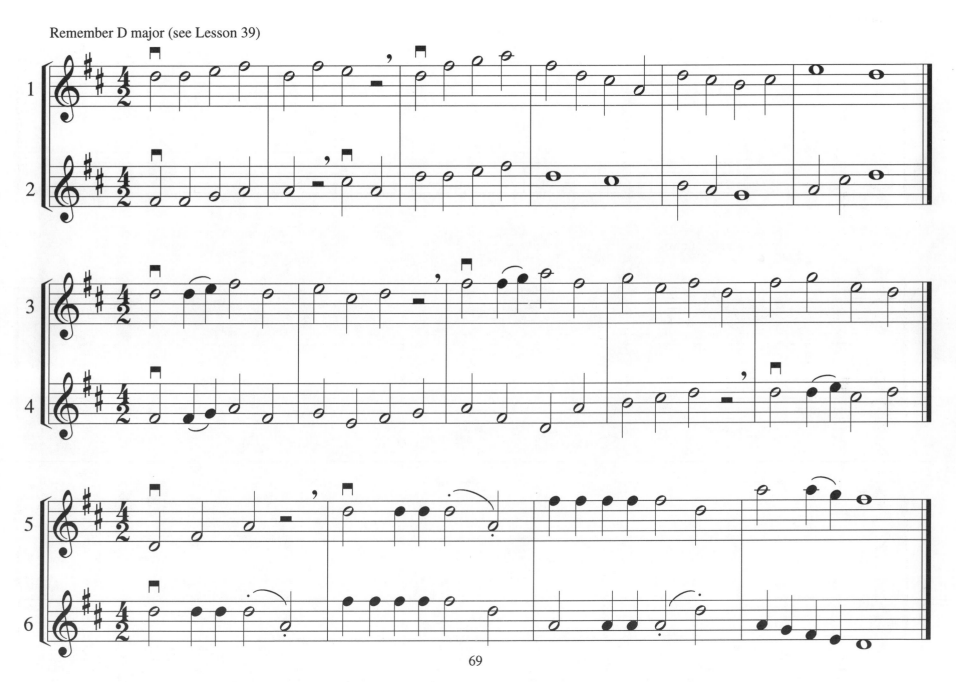

69

Lesson 65

In A major scale
    High 3 on G and D strings (for C# and G#)

70

Lesson 66

71

Lesson 67

In A major scale two octaves
High 3 on G and D strings (for C# and G#)
Regular 3 on A and E strings (for D and A)

72

Lesson 68

Remember - in A major
   High 3 on G and D strings (for C# and G#)
   Regular 3 on A and E strings (for D and A)

73

Lesson 69

The rest of this page is one duet
Read ahead when you reach the end of the line

Lesson 70

In D major
Regular 3 on A and D strings (for D and G)
High 3 on G string (for C#)

Lesson 71

Remember - in D major
  Regular 3 on A and D strings (for D and G)
  High 3 on G string (for C#)

76

In $\frac{3}{8}$ = $\frac{3}{\flat}$ Count 3 beats to a bar

An eighth note gets one beat

Count 3 beats to a bar in $\frac{3}{4}$ and $\frac{3}{8}$ *

Each pair of lines sounds the same

Lesson 72

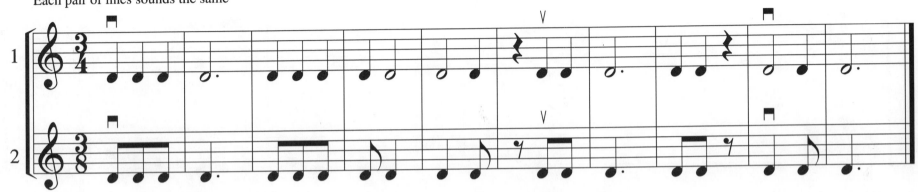

* At a quick tempo $\frac{3}{8}$ may feel like 1 beat to a bar

77

Lesson 73

The rest of this page is one duet
Read ahead when you reach the end of the line

Lesson 74

79

In 4/8 = 4/4 Count 4 beats to a bar
An eighth note gets one beat

Count 4 beats to a bar in 4/4 and 4/8

Each pair of lines sounds the same

Lesson 75

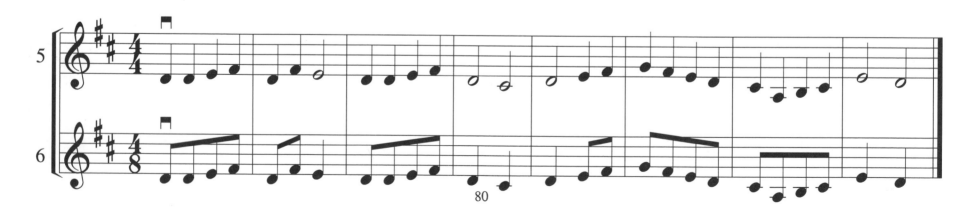

Lesson 76

81

Lesson 77

Remember G major (see Lesson 27)

82

Lesson 78

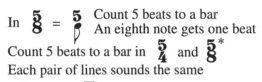

In $\frac{5}{8}$ = $\frac{5}{\flat}$ Count 5 beats to a bar
An eighth note gets one beat

Count 5 beats to a bar in $\frac{5}{4}$ and $\frac{5}{8}$*

Each pair of lines sounds the same

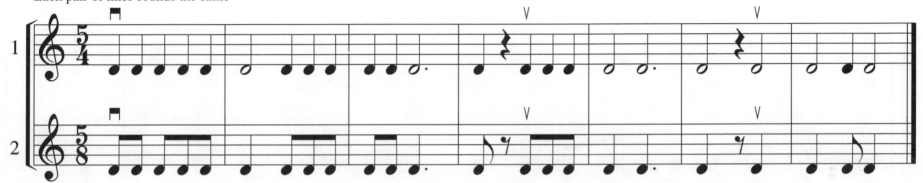

*Think of $\frac{5}{8}$ as two uneven beats per bar ♩♩ ♩♩♩ or ♩♩♩ ♩♩

83

Lesson 79

Remember C major (see Lesson 48)

84

Lesson 80

85

Lesson 81

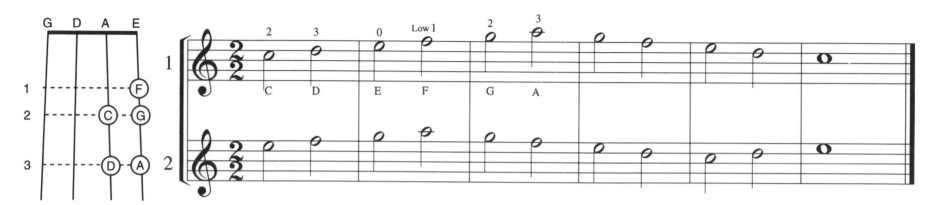

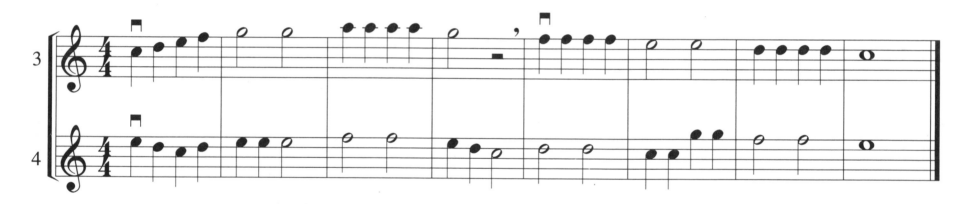

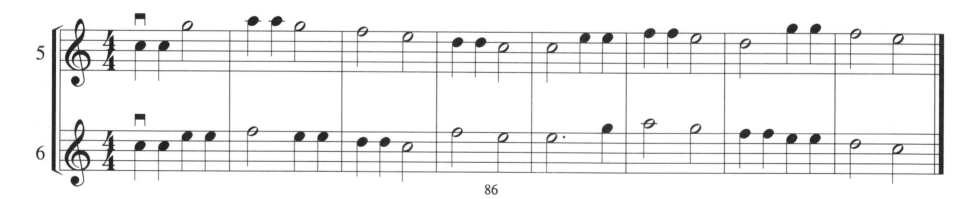

86

Lesson 82

Remember - in C major
 Low 1 on E string (for F♮)

87

Lesson 83

In F major scale
Low 1 on A and E strings (for B♭ and F)

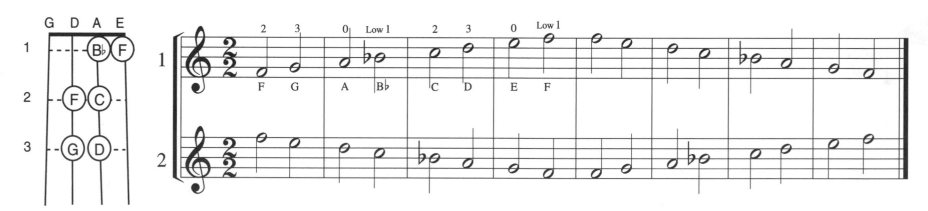

The key signature of F major has 1 flat (B♭)

Lesson 84

Remember - in F major
    Low 1 on A and E strings (for B♭ and F)

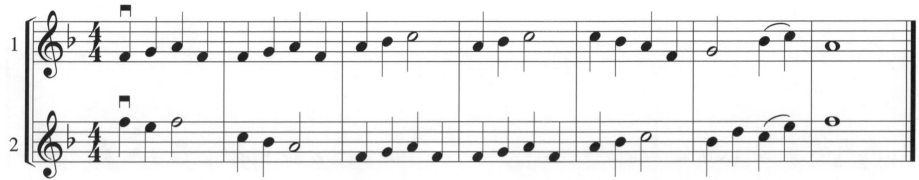

Lesson 85

Remember - count 2 beats to a bar in 2/2

90

Lesson 86

Remember - count 3 beats to a bar in 3/2

91

3 triplet eighth notes = 1 quarter note

The 3 is not a fingering - it means triplet

Lesson 87

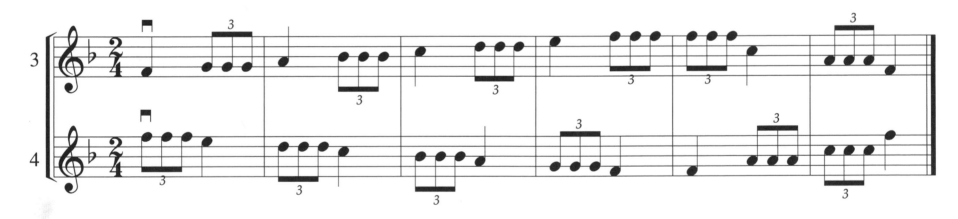

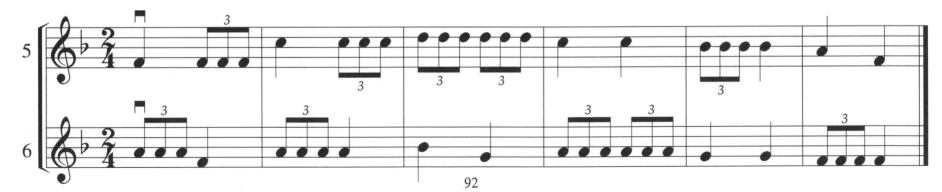

In $\begin{matrix}6\\8\end{matrix}$ = $\begin{matrix}2\\\text{♩.}\end{matrix}$ Count 2 beats to a bar
A dotted quarter note gets one beat

Count 2 beats to a bar in $\begin{matrix}2\\4\end{matrix}$ and $\begin{matrix}6\\8\end{matrix}$

Each pair of lines sounds the same

Lesson 88

Lesson 89

Remember - count 2 beats to a bar in 6/8

Remember G major (see Lesson 27)

Lesson 90

Remember D major (see Lesson 39)

95

Lesson 91

96

Lesson 92

Notice the rhythms

97

Lesson 93

Remember G major (see Lesson 27)

98

Lesson 94

Lesson 95

In C major
Regular 1 on D and A strings (for E and B)
Low 1 on E string (for F♮)

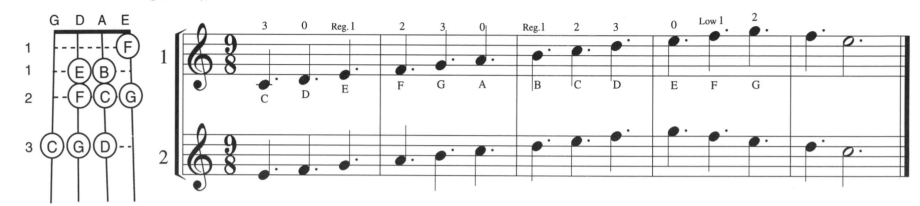

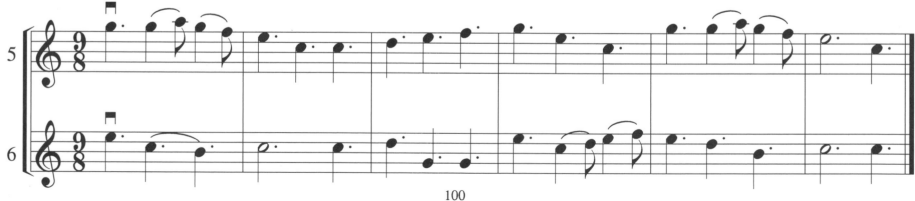

100

Lesson 96

Remember F major (see Lesson 83)

Lesson 97

In 12/8 = 4 Count 4 beats to a bar
A dotted quarter note gets one beat

102

Lesson 98

Remember C major (see Lesson 48)

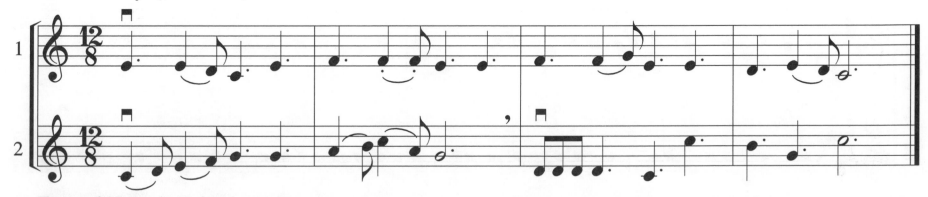

The rest of this page is one duet
Read ahead when you reach the end of the line

This page is all one duet
 Read ahead when you reach the end of the line

Lesson 99

Remember G major (see Lesson 27)

Lesson 100

This page is one duet
Read ahead when you reach the end of each line

105

Joanne Martin has been involved in the Suzuki movement since 1970, and has taught violin and viola in Edmonton, Vancouver and Winnipeg. For many years she was Coordinator of the University of Manitoba Suzuki Program, and now teaches violin and viola in her private Suzuki studio in Winnipeg.

Born in Winnipeg, she graduated with a B.A. from the University of Winnipeg, and has performance diplomas on piano (A.R.C.T. and A.M.M.) and viola (L. Mus.). She has played viola in the Winnipeg Symphony, Manitoba Chamber Orchestra and a number of other orchestras in Western Canada.

She is registered as a violin teacher trainer with the Suzuki Association of the Americas and has taught violin and Suzuki pedagogy for the School of Music, University of Manitoba.

Chamber music is one of her special interests; she performs regularly with the Concertante Chamber Players and has directed a String Chamber Music workshop at the University of Manitoba each summer since 1982.

She frequently teaches at Suzuki workshops and institutes, and has been a guest clinician in the United States, Canada, England, and France.